SCIENCE WORLD

EVERYDAY CHEMICALS

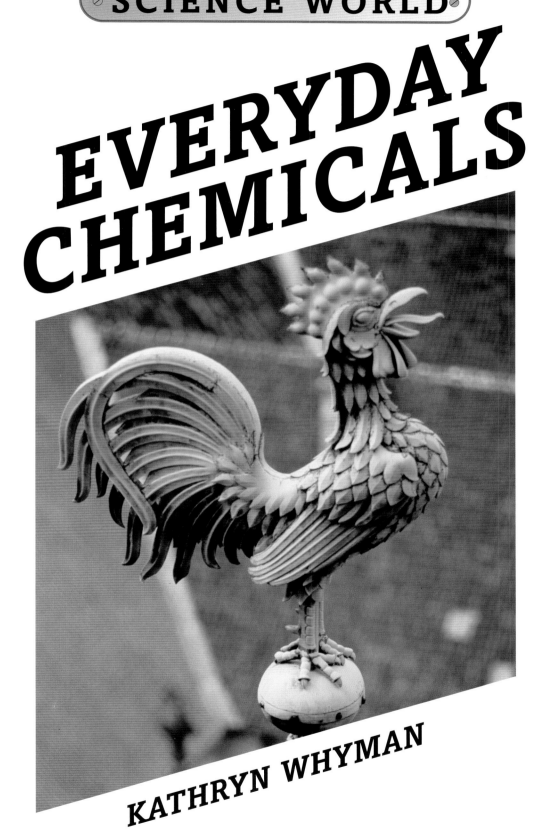

KATHRYN WHYMAN

Franklin Watts
London • Sydney

© Archon Press 2004

Produced by
Archon Press Ltd
28 Percy Street
London W1T 2BZ

New edition first published in
Great Britain in 2004 by
Franklin Watts
96 Leonard Street
London EC2A 4XD

Original edition published as
Simply Science – Everyday Chemicals

ISBN 0–7496–5548–8

Printed in UAE

Editor: Harriet Brown

Designer: Pete Bennett – PBD

Picture Researcher: Brian Hunter Smart

Illustrator: Louise Nevett

A CIP record for this book is
available from the British Library.

CONTENTS

INTRODUCTION

Everything that exists – from the Sun in the sky to the centre of the Earth, and from animals to vegetables – is made up of chemicals. Many of these are familiar to us, such as water, salt, sugar, iron and oxygen. Chemicals can be different from each other in many ways. They have different tastes, like sugar and salt, or different appearances, like gold and silver. Chemicals come in many different forms; some are solids, others are liquids or gases.

Oil contains many different chemicals. It is extracted from deep within the Earth.

In this book you will learn about the different physical and chemical properties of a range of substances. You will discover how a chemical can exist as a solid, liquid or gas and find out that some substances are made of one or two chemicals whilst others are made up of a large number. Find out how graphite in a pencil is actually made of the same chemical as a diamond and see how chemicals affect every aspect of our everyday lives.

Ice is made of chemicals.
It is the solid form of water.

THE CHEMICAL WORLD

Our world is composed of thousands of different substances. We call these substances 'chemicals'. Chemicals make up the air we breathe, the ground we walk on and the food we eat. Even our bodies are a collection of chemicals!

Chemicals are often put into groups. Water, salt, sugar and oxygen are all chemicals. We call them 'natural' chemicals. Plastics, detergents and cosmetics are everyday chemicals too. But these do not occur naturally – they are 'man-made'. Both types of chemicals are useful. Man-made cleaning agents remove dirt from our clothes and natural dyes from plants are used to colour fabrics.

Water is made of chemicals and without it there would be no life on Earth.

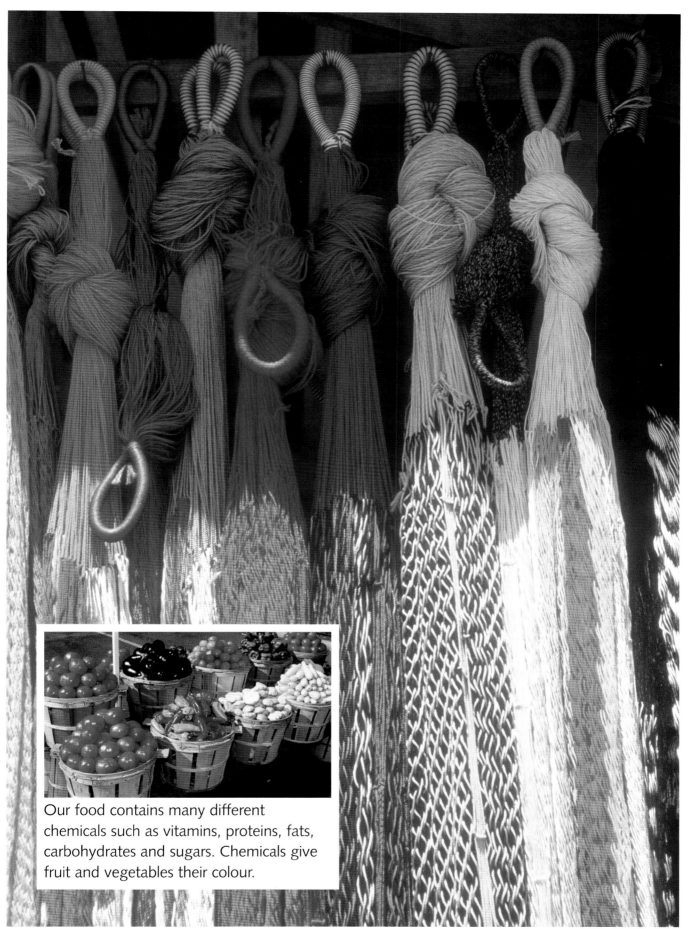

Our food contains many different chemicals such as vitamins, proteins, fats, carbohydrates and sugars. Chemicals give fruit and vegetables their colour.

Wool and cotton can be dyed with man-made chemicals or with natural chemicals from plants.

WHAT ARE CHEMICALS?

There are about 100 special chemicals called 'elements'. These are substances that cannot be broken down into simpler chemicals. The gases oxygen and hydrogen are both elements, so are iron and gold. Every element is made up of tiny particles called 'atoms', which are much too small to see, even with a microscope. Oxygen is composed of oxygen atoms, iron is made up of iron atoms.

Atoms can join together to make 'molecules'. A molecule of an element is formed from only one type of atom. For example, oxygen exists as a molecule of two oxygen atoms joined together.

Combining chemicals

When two different elements combine, they often make a compound which is very different from either of them. The element sodium is a shiny metal. The element chlorine is a green and poisonous gas. Sodium atoms and chlorine atoms can combine to make a very familiar compound – salt! However, we do not make the salt we eat by combining sodium and chlorine. The photograph opposite shows salt being produced from sea water. In cooler countries, salt is mined from underground.

Sodium

Chlorine

Salt
(Sodium chloride)

The atoms of one element may join up with the atoms of another element. When this happens, a completely different chemical is formed. For example, when two hydrogen atoms join with an oxygen atom, they make a molecule of water. Chemicals that are made by combining two or more elements are known as 'compounds'. Water is a compound. Sugar, salt, plastics – in fact, most of the chemicals around us – are compounds. A compound usually has different characteristics to the elements from which it is made.

Plastic is a compound of many different elements.

The salt that we eat can be obtained from sea water.

SOLIDS, LIQUIDS AND GASES

Chemicals may be solids, liquids or gases. Water is a liquid. When water is cooled to below 0°C it freezes and forms ice, a solid. When it is heated to 100°C it boils and changes to steam, a gas. We say that water can change its 'state'.

A chemical's state depends on its temperature. Solids may turn to liquids and gases and then back to solids again, as the temperature rises and falls. We usually see metals and rocks in their solid state. When they're heated, they become softer. If they're heated to a high enough temperature, they melt and become liquid.

Ice
Because the molecules in a solid, such as ice, are held firmly together and can only move about a fixed point, they have a definite shape.

Water
As a liquid, water molecules can move around more freely. The 'shape' of the water depends on the container.

Water vapour
The molecules in steam can move freely in all directions, spreading further and further apart until they fill their container.

In the Arctic, the temperature is so cold that sea water freezes into huge solid glaciers.

Steam is given off by cooling towers. The water vapour molecules move freely and spread apart.

CHEMICAL CHANGE

When water changes its state, its molecules are still made of hydrogen and oxygen – the chemical itself has not changed. When elements combine to make a compound, new molecules are formed. This is a 'chemical change'.

We see examples of compounds forming every day. Most metals combine with chemicals in the air. Copper roofs slowly turn green as the copper combines with water and oxygen to form a new compound. An iron nail left outside soon starts to turn brown. The iron has reacted with water and oxygen in the air to form 'rust'. Cars are made of several metals including iron. They have to be coated in paint to try to prevent them from rusting.

Baking a cake
When you bake a sponge cake, one of the ingredients used is baking powder. As it is heated in the oven, the baking powder breaks down into different chemicals.

One of these is a gas – carbon dioxide. The bubbles of carbon dioxide throughout the sponge make it light and fluffy. The baked sponge is now a new mixture of many different compounds.

Copper roofs slowly turn green as the copper combines with oxygen to form a new compound.

Iron bridges need to be coated with chemicals to prevent them from rusting.

SOLUTIONS

Salt 'disappears' in water. But a taste of the liquid tells you that the salt is still there. So what has happened to the salt? When salt is mixed with water, the sodium and chlorine atoms break away from each other and move freely in the water. Gradually, the sodium and chlorine atoms and the water molecules are mixed up evenly. The liquid is called a salt 'solution'. The salt has 'dissolved'.

Many substances dissolve in water. Water is a good 'solvent'. Carbon dioxide gas dissolves in water and makes it fizzy. Some substances dissolve in different solvents – paint dissolves in white spirit. Detergents 'help' water to dissolve oil.

Drops of oil floating on water will rush away from a drop of detergent added to the water. This is because detergent causes the surface of the water to change and the oil starts to dissolve.

Diffusion

If orange juice is poured down a straw into a glass of water, an orange patch forms in the middle of the water. The molecules of the water and the orange juice are moving all the time. Eventually, the orange molecules spread evenly throughout the water and the solution looks pale orange all over. This spreading of molecules is called 'diffusion'.

Sea water is a massive solution of salt and water.

Oil-based paint does not dissolve in water, but it will dissolve in a solvent called white spirit.

SEPARATING CHEMICALS

One way of separating chemicals is to use a 'filter'. A face mask is a type of filter. It is made of material that is full of tiny holes. Air can pass through these holes but particles of dust or paint are too big and get trapped on the outside of the mask.

A filter cannot separate salt from a salt solution. The sodium and chlorine atoms and the water molecules which form a salt solution are small enough to pass through the holes of any filter. If the solution is warmed, the water begins to change into vapour and eventually only salt is left behind. We call this process 'evaporation'. Stalagmites (shown right) form by evaporation.

Chromatography

There are three primary colours – red, blue and yellow. Most inks are made by mixing two or more of these colours. To separate ink, a process called chromatography is used. To try this yourself, draw a small circle on blotting paper using a water-based pen. Then put a drop of water on top of the circle. As the water spreads through the blotting paper, it carries the chemicals at different speeds and separates the colours.

Negative electrode

Electrolyte

Positive electrode

Battery

Electrolysis

Electrolysis is a process used to separate elements from compounds. An electrical current from a battery is passed through a liquid – called the electrolyte. Some molecules in the electrolyte are positively charged and others are negatively charged. Positively charged particles are attracted to the negative electrode. Negatively charged particles are attracted to the positive electrode. The liquid begins to separate. Electrolysis can be used to purify metals.

A face mask separates chemicals by preventing large particles from passing through the holes.

CRYSTALS

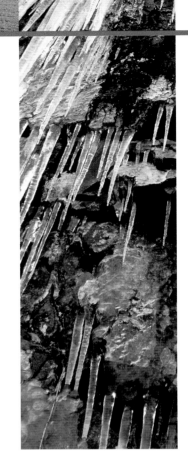

We have seen how to separate salt from a salt solution. If you look at salt under a microscope, you can see that each grain of salt is a perfect cube. The cubes form naturally as the salt comes out of solution. They are called salt 'crystals'. All salt crystals are the same shape, but they may be different sizes.

Many chemicals form crystals. Sugar makes crystals and so does water when it turns to frost or snow. Each type of crystal has its own shape. Most rocks are made of crystals of chemical compounds called 'minerals'. Granite is made up of crystals of 'quartz', 'feldspar' and 'mica'. Crystals of diamond or emerald may be made into jewellery.

Salt crystals

Salt is made up of an equal number of sodium and chlorine atoms. When salt is in solution, these atoms are far apart. But as the water evaporates, the atoms get closer together. They always arrange themselves in the same way. This arrangement, called a 'crystal lattice', gives the salt its cubic shape.

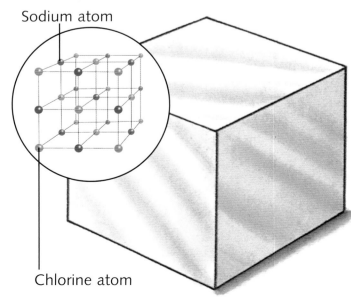

Sodium atom

Chlorine atom

Water crystals can form beautiful patterns.

Carbon

Carbon is an element: it is made up only of carbon atoms. But these atoms can arrange themselves in a number of ways to form several different types of carbon crystals. For example, charcoal is a soft black substance which can be used for drawing or may be burnt as a fuel; graphite is harder and is used to make the 'lead' in pencils. Surprisingly, diamonds are also pure carbon! Unlike charcoal and graphite, diamonds are extremely rare. They are used to make highly priced jewellery, and they also have industrial uses. Diamond is the hardest substance known and can be shaped to make cutting tools.

The graphite in pencil is made of carbon crystals.

Diamonds are also crystals of carbon. They are cut in a particular way to make them sparkle.

Acids and alkalis

Some chemicals are acids or alkalis. Vinegar, lemon juice and sour milk are all weak acids. They all have a similar sharp, sour taste. Oven cleaner, washing soda and toothpaste are all alkalis. Alkalis taste bitter and feel soapy.

Our stomachs contain hydrochloric acid. This acid kills some of the bacteria in our food and helps us to digest our meals. Too much stomach acid causes indigestion. Medicines used to cure stomach pains are often alkalis. When you mix an alkali with an acid, you make a 'neutral' solution – neither acidic nor alkaline. Many plants thrive in a soil which is not very acid, so farmers may add lime to the soil. Lime (an alkali) 'neutralises' acidic soil.

Acid rain, a form of polluted rain, is acidic enough to erode some stone statues.

Indicators

An 'indicator', such as litmus, is a substance that changes colour when it is mixed with an acid or an alkali.

When litmus paper is dipped into lemon juice, it turns red. Alkaline stomach medicine turns it blue. When the acid and the alkali are mixed, a neutral solution is formed which does not colour the litmus.

Car batteries contain a very strong acid solution. Never touch a car battery with bare fingers.

Farmers and gardeners use an alkali – lime – to neutralise acidic soil before planting.

CHEMICALS IN THE AIR

Air is a mixture. It contains many gases including nitrogen, oxygen and carbon dioxide. Nitrogen combines with other elements to make compounds called 'proteins'. Proteins help plants and animals grow, and animals need oxygen to breathe. At the top of a mountain, there is less air than at the bottom. For this reason, mountain climbers sometimes need to take extra oxygen with them.

In sunlight, plants grow by combining carbon dioxide and water to produce more of the chemicals of which they are made. Gases in the air are being used all the time, but they never run out! The diagram below explains why.

The Gas Cycle

We take oxygen from the air, but put back carbon dioxide. Plants take carbon dioxide from the air and, during the day, put back oxygen. Plant and animal bodies contain nitrogen. When they die, this nitrogen returns to the air or soil. Oxygen, carbon dioxide and nitrogen are constantly recycled so we never run out!

Fighter pilots take their own oxygen supply with them as there is very little air at high altitudes.

Plants and animals depend on each other to produce the chemicals needed for survival.

CHEMICALS FROM OIL

Crude oil is a thick, black liquid found deep under the Earth's surface. It was formed millions of years ago from the bodies of tiny animals and plants which lived in the sea. Crude oil is a mixture of many very useful chemicals.

Crude oil is pumped up to the Earth's surface and is piped to a refinery. Here the different liquids are separated from each other. Some of the liquids, such as petrol and paraffin, can be used as fuels. Others are changed chemically to produce compounds, such as plastics and waxes. Chemicals that come from oil are contained in many of the things we use every day, such as plastic bags and bottles, drain pipes, and some window frames and carpets.

Petroleum, the chemical used to power most cars, comes from crude oil.

Crude oil is found deep under the Earth's surface and is then refined at the surface.

Distillation column

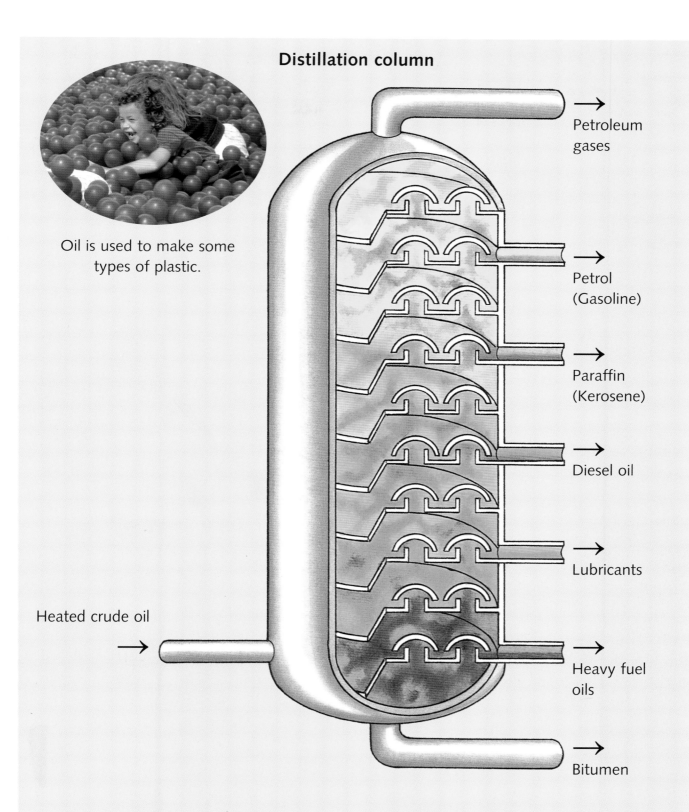

Oil is used to make some types of plastic.

Heated crude oil →

→ Petroleum gases

→ Petrol (Gasoline)

→ Paraffin (Kerosene)

→ Diesel oil

→ Lubricants

→ Heavy fuel oils

→ Bitumen

Each liquid chemical boils at a different temperature. The temperature at which it boils is called its 'boiling point'. When crude oil is heated at the refinery, its temperature slowly rises. The liquid with the lowest boiling point is the first one to boil and form a gas.

This rises upwards, then cools back to a liquid and is collected. As the heating continues, the liquids are separated and collected one by one. The last liquid to be collected is the one with the highest boiling point. This process of separation is called 'distillation'.

USES OF CHEMICALS

People have always used natural chemicals in their daily lives. Vegetable dyes are used to colour wool and cloth or to make paint. Other chemicals from plants have been used as medicines. Originally, drugs such as penicillin were made from moulds grown naturally. Today, most of our medicines are artificially produced.

Scientists have produced chemicals to help farmers. Fertilisers, spread on the fields, make crops plentiful and strong. Pesticides can be used to kill insects that damage crops. Although chemicals are used to improve our lives, many may be harmful too. For this reason, chemicals are developed and tested in laboratories before they are used.

Everything we use every day is made of chemicals.

Pesticides are sprayed on crops to protect them from being eaten by insects.

MAKE YOUR OWN INDICATOR

Red cabbage contains a coloured chemical which acts as an indicator. The blue dye from the cabbage turns pink in acids and green in alkalis. Neutral substances do not make the indicator change colour. Make your own indicator and find out which of the everyday chemicals you have at home are acids or alkalis.

What you need
Red cabbage, a knife, a chopping board, boiling water, 2 bowls, blotting paper, a wooden spoon, clothes pegs, string, milk, soap, lemon juice, bicarbonate of soda and water

Ask a grown-up to boil some water and chop the cabbage leaves. Put the cabbage leaves in a bowl.

Carefully add the water to the cabbage leaves. Stir the mixture using a wooden spoon. The dye from the cabbage will turn the water blue.

When the solution has cooled, pour the water into another bowl. You don't need the cabbage leaves anymore.

Dip strips of white blotting paper into the indicator solution. When they are soaked in dye hang them up to dry using string, tied between two points, and some clothes pegs.

Use your indicator paper to test any liquids you may have. (You can also test solids dissolved in water). Just place a few drops of each chemical onto a fresh piece of indicator paper. Try testing chemicals such as soap, milk, lemon juice, and bicarbonate of soda mixed with water. Different substances turn the paper different colours.

MORE ABOUT CHEMICALS

Chemicals surround us all the time and influence our lives without us even noticing. Here you can see a few more examples of some chemical and physical reactions with everyday chemicals.

Why not ask an adult to help you try some of them out for yourself?

Producing gas

Many different chemical reactions produce gas. At home, why not try producing carbon dioxide gas. To do this, mix together vinegar, which is acidic, and baking powder, which is alkaline, in a jar. Make sure the jar is in a sink – watch the bubbles of carbon dioxide erupt over the edge of the jar!

Physical change

Iron filings and sulphur can be mixed together. The iron filings can be easily separated from the mixture as they are attracted by a magnet. This is an example of a physical change. In a physical change, the material changes only its appearance. It is easy to reverse the change because no new substances are formed.

Chemical change

Eggs and bread are mixtures of compounds. When they are heated, new compounds are formed and a chemical reaction has taken place. We cannot undo this change in a simple way. Only complex chemical processes can reverse a chemical change.

How does evaporation work?

Ask an adult to help you boil a solution of salt and water. As the solution is heated, the tiny molecules move more rapidly. The water molecules eventually gain enough energy to fly off as gas. However, there's not enough energy for the salt to boil, and it is left behind.

GLOSSARY

Atom
A tiny particle. It is the smallest part of an element that can exist and still have all the characteristics of that element. It is the smallest unit of matter which can take part in a chemical change.

Compound
A substance consisting of two or more elements joined together. It cannot be broken down by physical changes.

Crystal lattice
The regular arrangement of atoms in a solid compound which gives it its characteristic shape.

Detergent
A substance which can be used to removed dirt and grease. Detergents are often man-made.

Diffusion
The gradual spreading of one material into another. Diffusion is quick in gases, slower in liquids and very slow in solids.

Dye
A coloured substance which can be firmly fixed to another substance. It cannot be removed by water or detergents.

Element
A substance which cannot be split into anything simpler by a chemical process, for example, iron or oxygen.

Erosion
The wearing down and breaking up of rocks by natural forces such as the wind, rain, ice, snow and running water. Acid rain can erode stone statues.

Fertiliser
A substance containing chemicals needed for healthy plant growth.

Litmus
A dye obtained from a type of plant called a lichen. It acts as an indicator to tell if a substance is acidic, alkaline or neutral.

Mixture
Two or more substances together which can be separated by simple physical means.

Molecule
Two or more atoms which exist as a group. A molecule is the smallest part of a compound which can exist on its own and still have all the characteristics of that compound.

Plastics
Compounds which contain carbon and whose molecules usually exist in long chains. These compounds often come from crude oil. Heat and/or pressure are involved in the manufacture of plastics.

Property
A characteristic which describes how a substance appears or behaves under certain conditions.

Reaction
The events which take place when two substances act on each other to produce new compounds.

Solution
When a substance dissolves in a liquid, we say it forms a solution.

Stalagmite
A column of calcium sulphate, usually seen growing up from the floor of a cave. Stalagmites are formed by a solution of water and calcium sulphate collecting on a surface. As the water evaporates, it leaves behind the calcium deposits.

INDEX

Photographic Credits

Abbreviations: l-left, r-right, b-bottom, t-top, c-centre, m-middle

Front cover main, front cover mt, back cover main, 6b, 17b, 20bl, 23b, 26tr — Corbis. Front cover mb, 4tr — Corbis Royalty Free. 1, 7 main, 13t, 16tr, 18bl, 25tl, 27 — Corel. 2-3, 5tr, 10tr, 11t, 18tr, 22tr — Digital Stock. 4tl, 6tl, 8tl, 10tl, 12tl, 14tl, 16tl, 18tl, 20tl, 21b, 22tl, 24tl, 26tl, 28tl, 30t, 31t, 32t — John Deere. 4-5, 11b, 12tr, 24b — Photodisc. 6tr, 24tr — Ingram Publishing. 7 inset, 28tr — USDA. 8tr, 21t, 26bl, 26br — Select Pictures. 9b — Bruce Coleman. 9tr, 13b — Flat Earth. 14tr — Rexam plc. 15t — Stockbyte. 15b — Brian Hunter Smart. 19b — Zefa. 20tr — PBD. 23t — US Air Force.